MEETING SCHOOLS OF ORIENTAL MEDITATION

MEETING THE OTHERS

MEETING SCHOOLS OF ORIENTAL MEDITATION by *H. E. W. Slade, S.S.J.E.*
MEETING JEHOVAH'S WITNESSES by *Jack Roundhill*
MEETING THE OCCULT by *Basil Wilby*

MEETING SCHOOLS OF ORIENTAL MEDITATION

by

H. E. W. SLADE
S.S.J.E.

LUTTERWORTH EDUCATIONAL
GUILDFORD & LONDON

First published 1973

LUTTERWORTH EDUCATIONAL   GUILDFORD & LONDON

ISBN 0 7188 2010 X

Printed in Great Britain by The Bowering Press, Plymouth

CONTENTS

PREFACE

KIPLING, who lived in India for many years and who absorbed so much of its spirit, wrote about its many religions in this way:

> All India is full of holy men stammering gospels in strange tongues; shaken and consumed in the fires of their own zeal; dreamers, babblers and visionaries: as it has been from the beginning and will continue to the end. (*Kim*, p. 45)

This picture is still true of the religious life of India. It has now been enlarged to include many other parts of the world, for there has been a large exodus of Indians and other Oriental people to the West, and these Eastern brothers have brought their many gospels with them. Not content with bringing these gospels, they have proclaimed them with such effect, that a growing number of Western disciples has gathered round them.

It is a common sight to find Oxford Street and King's Road enlivened by groups of enthusiastic imitators of Oriental religions, dancing in joyful procession before rather bewildered shoppers; and in America, where the hippie culture is more fully developed, this experience is even more varied, and on a larger scale. The 'stammering gospels' of the East have moved to the West and are being proclaimed, often by teachers who are still learning to adapt to their new and strange surroundings, and who have yet to master the language and ways of their European homes. By far the most effective instrument for this proclamation of the Eastern gospels to the West is the so-called Meditation School.

We should beware of adopting a too critical attitude towards these new teachers. In many ways they are imitating the efforts of past Western missionaries who exported their Christian Faith in an imitation Gothic form to a rather bewildered India. We have, all of us, much to learn from each other's mistakes.

The Oriental Meditation Schools which have grown up in the West are now numerous. They constellate around a particular faith or spiritual leader, and their emphasis is on the need for some form of training in the techniques of meditation. Many of these Schools are showing a remarkable ability to adapt their teaching to the needs of Western people. At the same time, many of them show a capacity to modify this teaching to their new surroundings. The Buddhist Society has admitted its intention of bringing into one the many forms of Oriental Buddhism, and hopes that out of this unification will grow a Western form of the Buddhist Faith.

Christians should not stand apart, indifferent to this religious activity. It is their duty to become informed and to discover how far they can co-operate with these Meditation Schools, and to find how much of their teaching and practice they can bring into their own prayer life. The Lambeth Conference of 1968 was aware of this need when it said that Christians had much to learn from the approach of Oriental religions to silence, and recommended that some religious communities might well explore forms of Eastern meditation.

To help Christians in this task we ask and try to answer the following questions about these Schools of Oriental Meditation: 1. What do they believe? 2. What have we to say? 3. What have we to learn?

H. E. W. SLADE, s.s.j.e.

Haywards Heath

1

WHAT THEY BELIEVE

ORIENTAL Meditation Schools in the West have their roots in the great Eastern religions of Hinduism, Buddhism and Islam. But no more than their roots. They have shown a remarkable capacity to assimilate other religions, and not least, Christianity. This description of the evening prayer at Gandhi's ashram of Sevagram is a typical example of the ease with which Indian religions have always been able to absorb truth from other Faiths:

> As dusk fell daily at Sevagram, the whole company of workers, old and young, teachers and pupils, gathered in orderly ranks on the ground, for evening prayers, a devotional period in which readings from Hindu scriptures, the singing of devotional songs, and silent prayer might well find a place along with the singing of a Christian hymn like 'Lead kindly light' and the recital of the Lord's prayer.[1]

However, in examining their teachings it will be best to group them around their parent religion, even though we shall find this Faith much modified by the various Meditation Schools. We shall first give an outline of the parent religion, and then the form it has taken in the derivative Meditation Schools. This method gives us three main groups of Meditation Schools: the Hindu, the Buddhist and the Islamic.

The Hindu Meditation Schools

Hinduism is the oldest of the Oriental religions and it exists in many forms. It is impossible to summarise its faith for unlike Christianity it has

[1] William Stewart, *India's Religious Frontier*, p. 62, S.C.M. Press.

no one creed. It is much more a way of life than a statement of faith, and this life is expressed in traditional rites, customs, mythologies, stories and country lore. Congregational worship on a large, organised scale is foreign to this religion, but there are great annual festivals such as Holi and Divali, largely connected with the natural seasons, and these are observed with great enthusiasm. Ashrams provide a community life which in some ways resembles the earlier forms of monasticism. The cow is a universal symbol of this religion.

Although Hinduism has no credal form, it has a varied literature, much of it written in the 'dead' language of sanskrit, and all of it requiring extensive editing and translation. This literature is divided into two main parts: the divinely inspired scripture (shruti) and the tradition (smriti).

The essential scripture is the *Veda* (wisdom), the literature brought into India by the invading Aryans, consisting of four collections of hymns which were used as a verbal accompaniment to religious sacrifices. They are: the *Rig-Veda*, the *Sama-Veda*, the *Yajur-Veda* and the *Atharva-Veda*. Closely related to this scripture are the compilations known as the Brahmanas and the Upanishads. From these hymns can be gathered much about the life and religion of India several thousands of years before Christ. It shows many differences from present-day forms of Hinduism and is a mine of quotations for those who would either reform the present religions, or create new ones.

The literature of the tradition is much more flexible and is of human composition. It includes the two great epics, the *Ramayana* and the *Mahabharata*. In the *Mahabharata* is included the Bhagavad-Gita which has been called 'the Bible of India' and is a major source of teaching in many Hindu Meditation Schools. These epics are very popular among the people and are used to communicate the main teachings of Hinduism to children. They supply the plots for much of the drama and the themes behind many of the dances.

The hymns are another part of the traditional literature. Among these may be included the Puranas, a collection of stories about the gods, which have inspired many of the hymns of the so-called bhakti cult. These hymns have been written by various authors such as Ramanuja (1175–1250), Chaitanya of Bengal, Mira Bai (b. 1504), Tulsidasa (b. 1532), Kabir (1440–1518), Tukaram (b. 1608) and a host of others. The tradition continues into the present day with the works of Gandhi, Tagore and Tilak. Many of the Oriental Meditation Schools draw on these hymns and the cult of Krishna on which so many of them are based for material in their vocal worship.

The other great literature of the traditional writings are the Yoga Sutras of Patanjali. Written about 200 B.C. they describe the discipline of Yoga as it was practised at that time. They are an invaluable exposition of the Oriental technique of contemplative prayer, and are perhaps the most important of all the sources employed by Oriental Meditation Schools in their teaching and practice of meditation. They have been adequately translated, and there is a number of commentaries available. However, the compact style in which they are written exposes them to a variety of interpretations, and many different forms of Yoga can claim Patanjali and his work as their authority.

In India, six philosophical systems have grown out of this literature. They are the Vaisheshika, the Nyaya, the Sankya, Yoga, Mimansa and Vedanta. The most important of them are the Vedanta and Yoga systems and it is from them that many of the present Oriental Schools of Meditation have compiled their own teachings. We shall group these schools therefore under the main headings of Vedanta and Yoga, with another division for the more independent Schools which have constellated round particular leaders who have claimed freedom to construct their own form of meditation.

The Vedanta Schools The Vedanta exposition of the *Veda* was largely the work of Shankara (A.D. b. 788). His teaching enabled Hinduism to become once more a living Faith in India and to replace Buddhism as the national religion. The six important principles of Vedanta teaching are:

(a) The transitoriness and unreality of the apparent world. This is signified by the word maya or illusion. This world has its origin in Brahman, but its visible form is a shadow of the real world as it exists in him.

(b) God is the supreme being and is known under the name of Brahman. He manifests himself as the true Self of man under the form called Atman. Man is destined to be absorbed in the divine being who inhabits the human heart. The phrase 'tat twam asi' (that thou art) sums up this part of the teaching which is called Advaita Vedanta. From time to time, Brahman manifests himself with special clarity through certain human beings called avatars.

(c) Karma is the inherited caste and character of every man. In Hinduism there are four castes: the *Brahmin*, the priestly caste; the *Kshetrya*, the military caste; the *Vaisya*, the merchant caste; the *Sudra*, the working caste.

(d) Reincarnation is the doctrine that a man is born into this world many times and in the form appropriate to his conduct and state of spiritual growth.

(e) Moksha, liberation from rebirth to union with God is the end of man's development.

(f) All religions are essentially one. It is this teaching which enables the Hindu to borrow from all religions and to use the Bible as another of his religious sources.

These principles, with infinite variations, form the basis of the teaching and practice of the Western Vedanta Schools.

Vedanta Schools of Meditation have grown up in many parts of the world, largely as a result of the inspiration of the Indian saint, Ramakrishna, who spent most of his life in the temple of Dakshineswar, near Calcutta. He died in 1886, having himself achieved enlightenment, and so inspired a group of able young man, led by Vivekananda, to develop and spread his teaching. They founded many centres of what is called the Ramakrishna Mission in India, which is devoted to contemplation and good works. In the West they founded the Ramakrishna Society with centres in England, America and the Argentine. Vivekananda, through his speaking and writing, achieved a remarkable success in communicating the Vedanta teaching to the West. In 1893 he addressed the World's Parliament of Religions in Chicago and laid in the West the foundation of his reputation as an exponent of Vedanta. His books on various forms of Yoga were popular and are still a valuable exposition of this way of discipline and prayer.

The Vedanta Schools in the West have shown much skill in adjusting their teaching to many Western religious forms and ideas. The Swamis draw freely on the New Testament, and they have imitated such services as Vespers in their corporate worship. They now conduct retreats for their followers in Christian retreat houses. At their centres, something like the monastic life is lived under the leadership of a Swami, and guests are welcomed in much the same way as in Christian religious houses. A genuine attempt is being made to understand the principles of Western thought, and as far as possible, to enlarge the Vedanta teaching to include them.

The meditation practised by these Schools is varied. They use mantras, symbols, vocal prayers and silence, and Indian forms of music with Indian instruments is popular. The meditations are usually done in groups but individuals are trained to discover the form which best meets their needs. Ramakrishna's teaching on the need to still the mind is one of the most important aims in the meditative training. He is reported to have said:

> In what condition of mind is the vision of God obtained? When the mind is perfectly tranquil. When the sea of one's mind is agitated by the wind of desires, it cannot reflect God, and then the God-vision is impossible.

In order to grow into this tranquillity of mind, certain of the Yoga postures are practised by some Vedanta Schools in the West.

These Meditation Schools are ecumenical in their teaching and practice. They do not require any renunciation of former beliefs, nor do they extract a detailed confession of faith from those who join them. For this reason many Christians have felt able to share their life without being conscious of disloyalty to their own Church.

The Yoga Schools Yoga is officially one of the six main systems of Hindu philosophy, but it is much more a technique of meditation training than an intellectual form of faith. It has been used in India for thousands of years, and was committed to writing in the mnemonic notes of the Yoga Sutras, by Patanjali in about 200 B.C. The Yoga Sutras are primarily the text-book of the meditation form of Yoga which is called Raja Yoga. There are other forms of Yoga for which other authorities are used: Hatha Yoga, a physical discipline, draws on the Hathayoga Pradipika; Karma Yoga, the way of God-directed work, uses the Bhagavad-Gita as its principle source; Vivekananda has written about Bhakti Yoga, the way of worship and Jnana Yoga, the way of study.

Yoga is practised today in India in many ways and is taught by individual gurus who each have their own interpretation. It varies from the organised forms taught in such a training school as is to be found at Lonaula, to the small village groups in all parts of India, where a kind of physical culture, with very little meditation, is the usual form. In fact, most Yoga exponents confine themselves to the physical side of Yoga and few move on to its meditation forms. There is a large body of itinerant Yogis who move about India and who settle sometimes in solitary places, and often at centres of pilgrimage. Like all other forms of spiritual expertise, Yoga has its charlatans who are concerned mostly with spectacular forms of physical control which this system undoubtedly brings.

Yoga discipline is divided into three parts. The initial training is concerned with regulations for the moral life, an essential foundation for all forms of meditation. The second part is a training of the body through certain physical postures, and the mastery of breathing techniques. The third part is a training of the heart for contemplation through the practice of concentration, meditation, and the mental tranquillity which leads to contemplation.

As a result of television programmes and expert propaganda, Yoga Schools have become numerous and popular in the West. These reflect the same variations as are to be found in their Eastern counterparts, and the most popular type at present is the Yoga for Health type of School which is mainly concerned with Hatha Yoga. These Schools attract many women, with their promise of prolonged youth and preserved figures. Small groups of Yoga practitioners, lightly organised, are to be found in almost every town. Sometimes these Schools provide simple meditation training, but the physical side of Yoga is their main interest.

There are signs that this kind of School has a limited life, unless it develops some other interest. Some Schools have moved into the occult and emphasise the esoteric teaching of Yoga, about the arousing of the spiritual centre of power called the kundalini. At present this type of School is not very numerous.

As in India, Yoga Schools form around an individual guru who usually puts his teaching into well-illustrated publications, a few of which have a wide sale. Much needs to be done in the way of translation and commentary before the compressed teaching of Patanjali is available for Western readers, in a form they can understand.

Independent Meditation Schools The essence of these Schools is that they have been founded and are controlled by a living teacher or guru, who demands a varying degree of obedience to his teaching from those who join his movement. In many ways these Schools are in the Bhakti or devotional tradition of Indian spirituality.

In 1968 considerable publicity was given to one of these Schools when the Beatles decided to join it. Two long articles, one in the *Observer* dated January 14, 1968 and the other in the American magazine, *Look*, of February 6, 1968, gave detailed accounts of this School and its leader. This was fortunate, for as Cyril Dunn in the *Observer* rightly noted 'No teacher will tell the outsider the exact nature of the technique. Nobody is given instruction until he has been ritually initiated.'

These Independent Meditation Schools have their roots in the Indian tradition of finding and following a guru. This guru-disciple relationship has been admirably described by Kipling in his great story, *Kim*. It is a relationship of deep and complete surrender and intimacy. It changes, when it comes to the West, in the number of disciples which accumulate around one guru. The two or three of the East become a vast multitude in the West, organised around sub-gurus, with all the communications expertise for which the West is famous.

Cyril Dunn in the *Observer* article gave this extract from the trust deed of the Meditation School he investigated:

> This School seeks the fulfilment of the purpose of the Christian religion, of leading people to the kingdom of heaven within in accordance with the teaching of Christ and by so doing to form a permanent connecting link between different religions.

Here we have a development of the Hindu ability to absorb other religions into itself in a rather exaggerated form. If this purpose were achieved, then this Meditation School would indeed be transformed into a Christian Church.

The position of the founder of this School and others like it is equalled only by the supremacy of the Pope over all members of the Roman

Catholic Church. He is an absolute source of teaching and authority. The claim to such leadership is based upon what is alleged to be a very special spiritual insight and experience. The guru is enlightened and does not need to make any appeal to a written and received tradition. As Schools of this kind grow and their founders become older and more remote figures, their presence will have to be increasingly mediated by others and through some kind of written tradition, if they are to survive.

The initiation rite into these Schools is simple yet with profound and lasting implications. It includes an exchange of incense and flowers and the gift of a word or mantra which, it is claimed, has been specially chosen to suit the particular needs of the candidate. This mantra is his special instrument of meditation; and the rite is supposed to establish a permanent relationship between the guru and his disciple.

Meditation is the chief activity of these Schools, although some meet the need for vocal prayer by introducing Eastern hymns and Eastern music. The meditation of one School was described to Paul Horn in this way:

> Transcendental meditation isn't new. It has been around for thousands of years; but periodically the technique becomes misinterpreted and lost until it is rediscovered and revived.

Apparently the technique is not difficult. It is claimed that it can be learnt in about fifteen minutes and consists in the repetition of the mantra until this becomes automatic and continuous.

One of the most attractive aspects of the meditation technique described to Paul Horn is the absence of any preliminary discipline such as is required in the teaching of Patanjali and the Catholic forms of meditation. The guru he interviewed said: 'I don't ask anyone to give up anything or live some special way: my message is, "Enjoy what you are."'

Some of these Independent Meditation Schools require more than this. They train their members through some forms of craft in recollection, and they make use of the Yoga postures.

The Buddhist Meditation Schools

Buddhism is a reformed version of Hinduism. It was founded by Prince Gautama who was born at Kapilavathu in north-east India in 563 B.C. When he came to manhood, he spent six years exploring religion, and he reached enlightenment under the bodhi tree at Buddha Gaya, in Bihar. As a result, he rejected the traditional form of Hinduism—the mantras, sacrifices, discipline and a Brahminical priesthood—and became a simple mendicant. He died in 483 B.C., having laid the foundations of a great religious Movement.

Buddhism spread rapidly after the Buddha's death, and with the support of Asoka (274–232 B.C.) became the state religion of India. It did not hold this position against a resurgent Hinduism led by Shankara in the ninth century, who replaced Buddhism with a revised form of Vedanta. But although Buddhism failed in India, it spread to other parts of the East and was able to vary its forms to meet the needs of other cultures. It split into two main forms at the beginning of the Christian era, the Hinayana or Theravada form, and the Mahayana or liberal form. Later in China and Japan it appeared as Zen, with an emphasis on meditation by the use of the koan, leading to a state of mental awareness known as satori.

Like our Lord, the Buddha left nothing of his teaching in writing. After his death, an enormous literature grew up around his life and teaching, with endless commentaries. The source of this literature is the Tripitaka or three baskets. These form the Pali canon, written about 80 B.C., and they are divided into: the Vinayapitaka, which gives the rules of Buddhist monks; the Suttapitaka, which records the sayings of the Buddha; and the Abhidhammapitaka, which contains the teaching of the Buddha on theology, psychology and ethics.

The essence of Buddhist teaching is summed up in the Three Jewels. These are the Buddha, the Dhamma, and the Sangha.

The *Dhamma* or doctrine is contained in the Four Noble Truths, the Noble Eightfold Path and the Five Great Precepts.

The Four Noble Truths are:

Dukkha, which mean frustration and pain and this is the great hindrance to man's happiness.

Samudaya, which is desire, the cause of pain.

Nirodha, which is the stopping of desire and the way to freedom.

Magga, which is the way of discipline which leads to the end of pain.

The Noble Eightfold Path is the way to wisdom, morality and mental peace. The way to wisdom is through right understanding and right thought. The way to morality is through right speech, right action and right livelihood. The way to mental peace is through right effort, right mindfulness and right concentration.

The Five Great Precepts are that one should refrain from injury to living things, from taking that which is not given, from sexual immorality, from falsehood and intoxicating liquors.

The *Sangha* is the monastic community in which Buddhism organises itself. The monks are bikkhus or mendicants. Their sole property consists of their robes, begging bowl, needle, a razor, and a filter to avoid taking life. Monastic regulations have multiplied. There are no rigid and life-long vows. Monks are always free to return to the world. Closely connected with the Sangha are the lay people, who share its weekly services and listen in silence to the chanting and reading by the monks. There are no sacrifices in this worship, although candles and flowers are sometimes given. The goal of Buddhism is Nirvana or spiritual fulfilment.

Unlike some other Oriental Meditation Schools in the West, Buddhism has clearly expressed its Faith and worship for Western people. One of the forms in which this is available is an explanatory booklet entitled *Buddhism and the Buddhist Movement Today*. This has been published by the Buddhist Society in London. In this publication are set out the basic Buddhist beliefs which have already been described, and also twelve agreed principles of Buddhism, which were promulgated in 1945. The following summary gives us the basic attitudes of this Western type of Buddhism.

1. Self-salvation is the immediate task for everyman.
2. Everything changes, except the flow of life.
3. This law of change applies to the soul.
4. The universe is the expression of law.

5. Life is one and indivisible.

6. The Four Noble Truths are: suffering, its cause and cure and the path to freedom.

7. The Eightfold Path is: right aims, speech, acts, livelihood, effort, concentration, samadhi and enlightenment.

8. Reality is indescribable and a God with attributes is not Reality.

9. From potential to actual enlightenment there lies the Middle Way, the Eightfold Path. This Way must be trodden by the whole man, the heart and mind must be developed equally.

10. Buddhism lays great stress on the need for inward concentration and meditation.

11. Buddhism knows no authority for truth, save the intuition of the individual.

12. Buddhism is a system of thought, a religion, a spiritual science and a way of life which is reasonable, practical and all-embracing.

This is a fair translation of Eastern Buddhism and the author expresses the opinion that 'from a fusion of divers Schools of Buddhism a Western Buddhism is being slowly born'. This must be a slow process and it is far too early to judge whether this hope is being fulfilled.

There are now many Buddhist centres in the West where teaching is given and meditation practised. For the meditation there are techniques for overcoming distractions, such as concentrating on breathing, walking and bringing the attention into focus on one point. It may be said that in this meditation there is little emphasis on God still less on his attributes and actions. The main end of the meditation training is to reach a state of complete inner harmony, leading to Nirvana or what the Zen Buddhists call Satori. Each meditator is under the guidance of an instructor, usually a monk of the community. Meditations are both corporate and individual. Some form of vocal prayer is used to supplement the meditation. This consists of chanting and the reading of the Buddhist scriptures, which is done by the monks whilst the congregation listens in silence. The ultimate goal of the meditative training is to lead the meditator to find his own way and the techniques which bring him to inner silence.

Since the invasion of Tibet by the Chinese, many Tibetan monks have come to the West and started their own med tation Schools. These are on a small scale and have not been going long enough to present us with a form of meditation which requires to be treated separately from the other Buddhist Schools.

The Islamic Meditation Schools

Islam is the name of the religion founded by Muhammad, a native of Mecca, born in A.D. 570. The word Islam means surrender or resignation, and those who follow this religion are called Muslims. Islam is a mono-theistic religion.

Muhammad was enlightened in A.D. 620 and when he began to teach, he was rejected by the people of Mecca. He retreated to Medina where he founded the Muslim era in A.D. 622. He died in that city ten years later.

Islam is the religion of a book, the *Qur'ān*. This is a collection of the teachings of Muhammad which is believed to have been divinely com-municated to him through an angel. From it are derived the teaching, worship and way of life of Islam.

The creed of Islam is summarised in the words: 'There is no God but God and Muhammad is the prophet of God.'

Four duties are required of the faithful: prayer (five times a day), alms-giving, observance of the fast of Ramadan and the making of the pilgrim-age (hajj) once during the lifetime of the faithful, to Mecca.

There is no caste system in Islam, all are equally brothers. The faithful are forbidden to eat pork and drink intoxicants. They bury their dead and treat marriage as a civil ceremony. Up to four wives are allowed.

The brotherhood among Muslims made them a strong fighting force and in early days they spread their religion by conquest, reaching France in 732 and only being narrowly repulsed by Charles Martel. Later they conquered India and held it until they were overthrown by the British.

Congregational prayer is the essence of Islamic worship. The crowded mosque, with its disciplined worshippers all performing their prostrations together and chanting in unison, is an impressive sight. Muslims venerate holy men and have a system for remembering their saints which resembles Christian commemorations. Painting and sculpture are officially forbidden in the mosque but this is often ignored. Islam is showing an ability to adapt many of its old rules to modern conditions.

Islam does not encourage non-Muslims to share its worship so that there are no Islamic Meditation Schools as such in the West. However, two movements have grown out of this religion, Sufism and Subud, and these are sufficiently liberal to be able to produce Meditation Schools suitable for the West.

Sufi Meditation Schools Sufism is a mystical movement within Islam which arose in Persia through a school of poets, which included the great Jala-ud-din-Rumi (1207–1273). Rumi wrote the Mathnawi, a collection of spiritual couplets which inspired many other poets and religious people to experiment with a less rigid form of religion than Islam, where much Hindu teaching could be included, and individual teachers allowed to propagate their own particular forms of prayer. In the 14th century the saint Ramanuja and the poet Kabir, both from India, added this Hindu element to the Sufi movement.

The more important principles of Sufism are:

There is one God.
Creation is an external manifestation of him.
God is both immanent and transcendent.
God most perfectly manifests himself in man.
The goal of religion is love.

Rumi sums up much Sufi teaching in this lovely verse:

Deep in our hearts the light of heaven is shining
Upon a soundless sea without a shore.
Oh, happy they who have found it in resigning
The image of all that men adore.

One of the fundamental teachings of Sufism is that all religions are essentially one since there is only one God and one truth. This accounts for the ecumenical attitude of this form of Islam both in the past, when it brought Muslims and Hindus together, and in the present through the teaching of such leaders as Inayat Khan who worked for the unifying of men of all Faiths in one loving experience of God.

Sufi Meditation Schools form around individual teachers who stamp them with their own particular views. One such School describes its purpose in this way:

21

It is a centre where young people of all ages can come for limited periods to receive the benefits of the teaching and healing available; a place to teach people to help people to make a better world.

It goes on to give details of week-end programmes which are variable and includes many activities geared to bring all to a greater understanding of love and awareness. One of the purposes of the training is to help people wake up to what they are in everything they do. Various practices and exercises in concentration are taught, and each day there is a period of meditation as well as a series of physical exercises and practices in group encounter.

At the Inter-Religious Congress organised by the Sufis under Pir Vilayat Khan in April 1969, the ecumenical aspect of Sufism was demonstrated when representatives of many religions came together and shared each other's Faiths.

Subud Meditation Schools Subud, another offshoot of Islam, came from the teaching of Pak Subuh, a Muslim from Malaya. He taught a simple theism and practised a spiritual process he called latihan or opening. This was a kind of induced mystical experience which was brought about by trained leaders who operated under the Spirit on those they considered ready for such experience. At one stage it was taken up by some of the followers of Gurdjieff, led by J. G. Bennett.

Subud manifests itself in small local groups, and in its spontaneous response to the Spirit has something resembling Pentecostalism. Since there is no clearly defined doctrinal teaching in these groups, people feel free to join them without compromising their relationship with their parent Church. The conduct of local meetings varies. Much is made of spontaneous movement and latihan is practised when people feel moved to do so. Prayers, silence and meditation are controlled by the Spirit.

In attempting to summarise the teachings of the various Oriental Meditation Schools, there is always the danger of leaving out some group, or of over-simplifying the teachings and practices of others. These Schools represent not a completed and past spiritual Movement but one that is in process of growing, and which is alive in the present. There must therefore be continuous movement in what has been described, and the Schools change even as we write and others read about them. But there are common areas between us which both enable us to understand each other and promise a growing co-operation in the future. These common areas are referred to by Bernard Lonergan in his book *Method in Theology*. He writes:

> There is at least one scholar on whom one may call for an explicit statement on the areas common to such world religions as Christianity, Judaism, Islam, Zoroastrian Mazdaism, Hinduism, Buddhism, Taoism. For Friedrich Heiler has described at some length seven such common areas.

He then goes on to summarise them as follows:

> There is a transcendent reality.
> He is immanent in human hearts.
> He is supreme beauty, truth, righteousness, goodness.
> He is love, mercy, compassion.
> The way to him is repentance, self-denial, prayer.
> The way is love of one's neighbour, even of one's enemies.
> The way is love of God, so that bliss is conceived as knowledge of God, union with him, or dissolution into him.[1]

It is these common areas which assure us that we can grow in the understanding of each other. They also assure us that in trying to understand each other, we are bringing light from others to illuminate and clarify our own traditions.

[1] Bernard Lonergan, *Method in Theology*, p. 109, Darton, Longman & Todd, 1972.

2

WHAT WE HAVE TO SAY

JOHN MACQUARRIE, in his *Principles of Christian Theology*,[1] writes about commitment and open-ness in religion. He rejects the often-held view that one religion is true and all the rest false. He appeals for an opening-up of the Catholic view, and says that 'the time has come for Christians to have a far more open and generous attitude towards other faiths.' In saying this he does not advocate syncretism. He argues that 'men should be loyal to their own tradition and sympathetic towards others'. He considers that 'religious pluralism will be with us for a long time if not for ever', and urges that religions should not only find a *modus vivendi* but should also seek closer understanding of each other.

Vivekananda said much the same thing in his book on Bhakti Yoga. He wrote:

> The bhakta must take care not to hate, nor even criticise, those radiant sons of light who are the founders of various sects; he must not even hear them spoken ill of. [He then goes on to quote Tulsidas:] 'Take the sweetness of all, sit with all, take the name of all, but keep your seat firm.'[2]

Already this important lesson had been taught by our Lord. 'Do not stop him, for who is not against you is on your side.' (Luke 9: 50.)

We live in what might be called the ecumenical age of Church history, but unless our interpretation of ecumenism stretches out beyond our domestic divisions to the whole inhabited world, making us eager to talk

[1] pp. 155–8, S.C.M. Press, 1966.
[2] *Bhakti Yoga*, p. 56, Advaita Ashram, 1964.

on equal terms with the great non-Christian religions, it will be a starved and puny thing. The Oriental Meditation Schools in our midst provide us with an immediate opportunity to stretch our ecumenism. They call us to a closer and more loving understanding of each other and to the adventure of finding a *modus vivendi*. This is not a call to a vague compromise or forced syncretism. It demands that we shall keep our seat firm in our own particular tradition, and then constructively and critically approach the meditation traditions of these Oriental systems.

In this section we shall attempt to do this both negatively and positively. This will involve us in first of all presenting an outline of our own Christian meditative tradition, and then considering the important ways in which the Oriental Meditation Schools differ from it. We shall then pass on to examine the ways in which we can positively approach these Schools and learn from them ways in which to enrich and clarify our own tradition.

The Christian Meditative Tradition

There have always been many Schools of Meditation within the Christian Church. In the Bible we find different people meditating in different ways. Our Lord on the Mount of Transfiguration meditated in the presence of the Father. St. Stephen at the time of his martyrdom meditated on the glorified Christ, and committed his life to him. St. Paul describes many other ways of meditation. St. Peter on the roof of his friend's house uses mental images of unexpected forms. The Church has always been able to hold in balance the many different ways of meditation used by her children. It has always been like this and will probably go on like this till the end of time. Meditative pluralism, to adapt the words of John Macquarrie, will be with us for a long time, if not for ever.

But this does not mean that behind these many forms there are not certain common principles. Such principles exist, and they are expressed with profound unanimity, both in scripture and the traditions of the Church, and in the lives and teaching of an innumerable host of her children.

Scripture is the fundamental source of these principles, but here they are to be found with much other material, and without systematic form. It is in the traditions of the Church and especially her prayer forms that

C   25

these Bible principles are presented to us in a selected and ordered form. When we come to formulate them, we shall make particular use of the Holy Communion as the clearest and most generally used source of this tradition.

Mention has been made of the innumerable host of meditators within the Church through all ages. We have already used the lives and teachings of individuals to discover the principles of Eastern meditation. The lives and teachings of Christians are equally the best way of discovering the principles of Western meditation. But their name is legion, and at this stage we can do no more than mention some of the outstanding people who have taught and developed the many ways of Christian meditation. Through their biographies more may be learnt about this form of prayer than through any other way.

First, the Desert Fathers, a great host of men of prayer, among whom was St. Anthony (285–356). Their life and prayer have been described by Cassian in his book called *The Conferences*.

Then there were the founders (360–435) of the early religious communities, St. Pachomius (292–348), St. Basil (329–379), St. Benedict (480–542), St. Bernard (1090–1153), Hugh of Saint-Victor (d. 1141), Richard of Saint-Victor (d. 1173).

Standing apart from these and in a tradition of his own was St. Ignatius Loyola (1491–1556). His Spiritual Exercises organised the discursive form of meditation into a kind of training which had an immense influence on the whole Christian Church.

And finally, the great national groups:

The Spanish Mystics—St. Theresa (1520–1582), and St. John of the Cross (1542–1591).

The French School led by St. Francis de Sales (1567–1622).

The Italian Mystics—Lorenzo Scupoli (1530–1601), and St. Catherine of Genoa (1447–1510).

The English Mystics of the 14th Century—Walter Hilton (d. 1396), Julian of Norwich and the author of the *Cloud of Unknowing*.

These are no more than a few of the many who could be mentioned. They have left behind them a great legacy of prayer and ways of contemplation.

The Holy Communion is the main instrument of Christian corporate prayer. It takes many forms in different Churches, but underlying them all are three controlling principles, which are also the principles of Christian meditative prayer. These are that the energy of prayer is the Holy Spirit, the centre of prayer is the Lord Jesus Christ, and the end of prayer is loving union with the Father. These principles are expressed in the form of Holy Communion called Series II, now widely used in the Church of England.

The Inspiration of the Holy Spirit The Holy Communion begins with this prayer:

> Almighty God, unto whom all hearts be open, all desires known, and from whom no secrets are hid: cleanse the thoughts of our hearts by the inspiration of thy Holy Spirit, that we may perfectly love thee, and worthily magnify thy holy Name; through Jesus Christ our Lord.

This prayer states the first essential principle of Christian meditation. It is an activity made possible through the energising presence of the Spirit of God. He comes, as we pray, to strengthen all the faculties of man. He renews the body by transforming it into the spiritual body. He renews the heart by cleansing it of all hindrances, and energising it with his light and love. The Spirit begins the activity of meditation and man co-operates with him. This is both humiliating and encouraging. Without God we can do nothing: with him all things are possible. During those stages of prayer when the natural faculties dry up, this truth brings us the confidence to persevere. The so-called Dark Night of prayer is inevitable for those who would penetrate through to God, but with the help of the Spirit who lightens this darkness, there is nothing to fear.

The Centrality of Christ The Holy Communion makes it clear that the centre of this prayer is Christ. Christ is presented in this service in many ways. He is presented, by means of words, in the section described as The Ministry of the Word, and in the section called The Communion, through the signs of bread and wine.

III.13

I.1

I.2

I.4

III.14

III.15

V.22

VI.25

VI. 27

IV.19

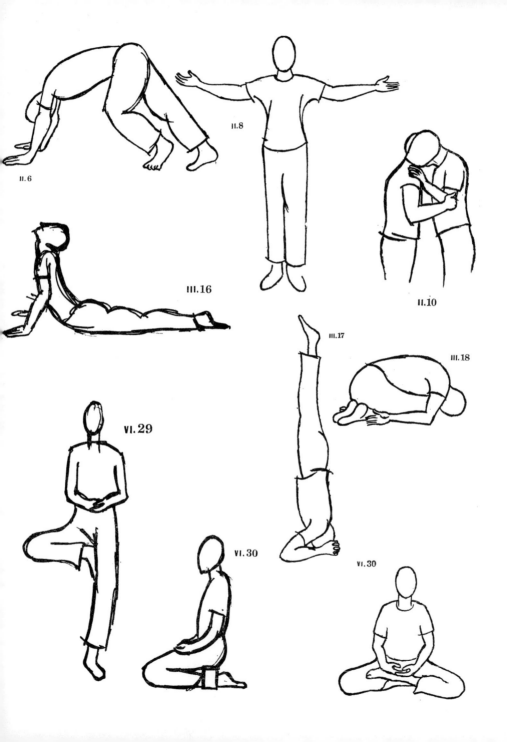

II.6

II.8

II.10

III.16

III.17

III.18

VI.29

VI.30

VI.30

The Ministry of the Word is made up of (a) three readings from the Bible (an Old Testament lesson, the Epistle and the Gospel), and (b) a commentary in the form of a sermon and the creed. The readings are chosen to present the great events and teaching of Christ as they are summarised in the Creed, that is, the mysteries of his incarnation, his ministry, crucifixion, death, resurrection and ascension, and the continuation of his work through the Holy Spirit. These events are still further emphasised by the festivals by which they are commemorated every year at Christmas, Lent, Holy Week, Easter, Ascension and Pentecost.

The Christ of the Holy Communion is the Christ of the scriptures. This is much more than an historical portrait to be understood by reason. It is the mystery of faith which is appropriated by contemplative prayer. The mystery is given in the carefully chosen stages known as the incarnate mysteries, and the faithful are trained not merely to know them as events recorded in the Bible, but to enter into them so completely that they grow to reproduce them, both in themselves and in the events of their daily lives.

The Christ of the Holy Communion is also the Christ of tradition and tradition is the answer of every age to the question: 'What think ye of Christ?' The answer is given both in the present and in the past and without contradiction. The present answer in the Holy Communion is given through the sermon: the past answer through the Creed. In this tradition Christ is described in terms of perfect God and perfect Man, as the divine person who took the whole manhood into himself and in so doing, restored our humanity and raised it to participate in the life of God. This traditional interpretation of the living Christ may seem unnecessarily detailed and complicated, but this precision is needed when he is used as the centre of meditative and contemplative prayer. We can only safely say with St. Catherine of Genoa: 'My me is God, nor do I know my selfhood save in Him', when we have firmly grasped the total mystery of Christ as given through the Ministry of the Word in the Holy Communion. Through the guide-lines given, we can avoid the dangers of pantheism, and of self-annihilation, in the form of a death-dealing quietism.

The Christ of tradition is both past, present and future. There is a place for other insights outside of the Bible in the growth of this tradition. To this William Temple referred when he wrote:

All that is noble in non-Christian systems of thought or conduct or worship is the work of Christ upon them and within them. By the Word of God—that is to say by Jesus Christ—Isaiah and Plato and Zoroaster and Buddha conceived and uttered such truths as they declared. There is only one divine light; and every man in his measure is enlightened by it.[1]

In the section called 'The Communion', Christ is communicated with under the signs of bread and wine. This may be described as the image form of presenting Christ, as compared with the form of communicating with him through words. It requires the response of loving faith, in terms of a total use of the faculties of the heart, in terms of imagination, understanding and love. The gift of the bread and wine is accompanied by the command to feed on him in the heart by faith with thanksgiving.

This image-mode of presenting Christ has important implications in the reception of him in mental prayer. It points to a development of that prayer, through meditation to contemplation, from the penetration of faith, to the union of love.

The means by which we grasp the total mystery of Christ is faith working by love, and in the Holy Communion, this faith is guided both by words and images, the ministry of the Word and the Communion. In using all these instruments the Church aligns herself to the broad tradition that the opening of the heart to the spiritual world requires the use of all our faculties, under the direction of a God-given faith. In this way Christ is presented not merely as a central figure of the past, which in our meditations we recall, but as the central figure of the present, whom we assimilate as we feed on him in our hearts, by faith and with thanksgiving.

Union with the Father in Christ The climax of the Holy Communion is the Lord's prayer. This is addressed to the Father, and in Christ we approach him as adopted sons, sharing in his divine Being. This stresses the end of contemplative prayer. It is the Godhead, symbolised by Christ in the image of Father which conveys the truth that the Godhead is more than pure Being or holy Being: he is loving Being with whom his sons may attain a loving communion. Becoming identified with Christ in the

[1] *Readings in St. John's Gospel*, p. 9, Macmillan, 1963.

31

centre of our being is much more than becoming like him and sharing his perfect human nature. It is a participation in the divine nature. This is one of the main points where Christian meditation parts company with the advaitism of Vedanta teaching, for in this union, we do not lose our humanity any more than our Lord lost his. By sharing the perfection of the Lord's humanity we become capable of sharing his divinity, without becoming annihilated in the process. It is as sons that we find our loving union with the Father. This is an essential principle of Christian meditation which is clearly stated and practised in the Holy Communion, where we not only share in the life of the incarnate Son but in him penetrate to the abyss of the Godhead, as he leads us to share in his union with the Father.

Some Defects in the Oriental Schools Meditative Tradition

When we compare the Oriental Schools meditative traditions as they are taught and practised at this time in the West, there are many and obvious differences between them and our Christian traditions. We must beware not to interpret all of these differences as defects. The more open-minded we are to them, the more likely we are to find that many differences are but other ways of saying the same thing, and that from them we have much to learn. Yet there are defects, and it is our duty to recognise two of them, not in any over-critical way, but in order to avoid repeating the mistakes of past Christians who have also made them. These Christians tried to become self-sufficient, masters of their fate and captains of their souls, and found that this way led to failure and despair. Over many centuries they struggled with the mystery of Christ and made their mistaken answers, from the demi-god theories of Arius, to the God-absorbed conclusions of Eutyches.[1] Slowly the Church reached the conclusion that the Grace of God was an essential condition of prayer and that the mystery of Christ was the union of the divine and human natures in One who is perfect God and perfect man, the 'focus of Being' who alone can meet all

---

[1] Arius and Eutyches were Christian teachers in the early 4th Century. Arius said that Christ was not divine and his teachings were condemned by the Church at the Council at Nicea (A.D. 325). Eutyches said that Christ's human nature was lost in the divine. His teaching was condemned at the Council of Chalcedon (A.D. 451).

our needs. In many of the Oriental Meditation Schools there are signs that these mistakes in other forms are still being made and they form the two main defects it is our duty to criticise. They are an inadequate teaching about the grace of the Spirit and an uncertainty about the place and Being of Christ in the life of contemplation.

Inadequate Teaching about the Grace of the Spirit In the early centuries of the life of the Christian Church there was considerable tension between two theories of the presence and work of the Spirit. The theory of Pelagius was that man by his own unaided will took the initiative in his own spiritual growth. The theory of St. Augustine, in opposition to this independence, was an insistence on the divine initiative in man's spiritual life and the need for our wills to be assisted. But Augustine went too far and developed theories of predestination and irresistible Grace which undermined the reality of man's free will, and therefore of his capacity to love. Undoubtedly St. Augustine was right in his main contention, but he overstressed the truth into an error. The true balance between the presence and work of the Spirit in man's spiritual life is accurately described in this collect:

> O God, forasmuch as without Thee we are not able to please Thee;
> mercifully grant that thy Holy Spirit may in all things direct and rule
> our hearts; through Jesus Christ our Lord.

This balanced teaching about the help of the Holy Spirit seems to be lacking in both the teaching and practice of many of the Oriental Meditation Schools.

Patanjali describes in admirable detail a technique for stilling the mind for contemplation, but what he regards as essential is the repetitive perseverance and detachment of his pupil. He leaves out any teaching about the initiative and co-operation of the Holy Spirit in this process.

The first of the Twelve Principles of Buddhism says that 'self-salvation is for any man the immediate task', but nowhere is there specific teaching comparable to the New Testament teaching about the Spirit, concerning the way in which God makes salvation possible.

Christopher Isherwood in his introduction to *Vedanta for the Western World* writes:

Reduced to its elements, Vedanta Philosophy consists in three propositions. First, that man's real nature is divine. Second, that the aim of human life is to realise this divine nature. Third, that all religions are essentially in agreement.[1]

Again there is in this summary no mention of the part God plays in making this realisation possible.

And Hazrat Inayat Khan writes of Sufism in this way:

> By the process of Sufism one realises one's own nature, one's true nature, and thereby one realises human nature, and by the study of human nature one realises the nature of life in general. All failures, disappointments and sorrows are caused by the lack of this realisation; all success, happiness and peace are acquired by the realisation of one's own nature. In short, Sufism means to know one's true being, to know the purpose of one's life and to know how to accomplish that purpose.[2]

This again is a very different approach to realisation from that of the Christian collect. The emphasis is on self-help. There is no mention of the initiative of God in the redeeming work of Christ and the sending of the Holy Spirit.

Our Lord taught us to judge inadequacies of this kind by their fruits and there are signs in Oriental Meditation Schools of two failures resulting from the absence of a full place for the Holy Spirit in prayer. They are an undue dependence on human guidance and recourse to artificial stimulants.

In many Oriental Meditation Schools the spiritual leader or guru assumes a place of first importance. He is much more than the spiritual director in Christian spirituality, whose function is to guide and not to dominate. The guru is much more like a dictator. He is the source of doctrine, of the meditation mantra, and of the individual control in which so many come to depend completely. Sometimes in the early stages this kind of leadership may help, but if it lasts too long the disciple remains undeveloped and fails to reach the spiritual independence of an adult.

[1] p. 9, Unwin Books, 1963.
[2] The Sufi Message of Hazrat Inayat Khan, *Vol ix*, p. 253, Barrie and Rockliff, 1963.

There are forms of Tantric Yoga in which the use of drugs and certain sexual techniques replace the traditional disciplines of meditation. These are condemned by the many Oriental Meditation Schools. But at present there are signs that some who are using Eastern forms of meditation are supplementing them with drugs and certain magical techniques which are supposed to hasten the experience of awareness and enlightenment. Aldous Huxley gave the support of his wide reputation to this way when he wrote his *Doors of Perception* and used mescalin. This use of drugs is of course discouraged by Patanjali, although he was aware of their possibilities. It is not that they fail to bring an experience; it is the damage they cause to the whole personality in giving it. Drugs used as a short-cut to meditation have a catastrophic effect on the mental balance of those who use them, and there are many examples of those who become over-dependent on them, adopting them as an antidote to despair and failure.

The Optional Christ Already we have quoted from the trust deed of one Meditation School which claims, as one of its purposes, 'the fulfilment of the purpose of the Christian religion of leading people to the kingdom of heaven within'. Many Meditation Schools give Christ an important place in their teaching, but He shares it with many other options, and the New Testament image of God in Christ is rivalled by a plethora of other images derived from Eastern ways of thought. Dr. C. G. Jung saw this confusion of the images from two very different traditions as a grave danger to mental stability. He wrote:

> Western man cannot and should not give up his Western understanding, on the contrary he should apply it honestly, without imitation, or sentimentality, to understanding as much of Yoga as is suitable.[1]

He spoke of the result as 'a stultification of our Western intelligence'.

The whole of Western Christian thought has been formed around the person and teaching of Christ. This is even more true of Christian contemplative prayer. His primal and exclusive place has been described by one of the greatest contemplatives, St. John of the Cross, who wrote:

[1] *Collected Works*, Vol. 11, p. 558.

For in giving us, as He did, His Son, which is His Word—and He has no other—He spake to us all together, once and for all in this single Word, and He has no occasion to speak further. . . . Wherefore he that would now enquire of God, or seek any vision or revelation, would not only be acting foolishly, but would be committing an offence against God by not setting his eyes altogether upon Christ, and seeking no new thing or aught beside. For He is my complete speech and my answer, and He is all my vision and all my revelation.[1]

Eastern spiritual leaders have always been willing to give Christ a place as one of many manifestations of God. Ramakrishna once used the Christian mysteries of Christ in his meditation, but he afterwards returned to other images. Gandhi had a great reverence for Christ and especially the Sermon on the Mount, but again he made him the equal of many others. In Oriental Schools of Meditation there is nothing parallel to the Christian demand that men should turn to Christ. There is nothing which approaches St. Paul's claim that in Christ 'the complete being of God, by God's own choice, came to dwell. Through him God chose to reconcile the whole universe to himself, making peace through the shedding of his blood upon the cross—to reconcile all things, whether on earth or in heaven, through him alone.' (Col. 1: 19–20)

Christians cannot compromise with this exclusive centrality of Christ by using forms of meditation which encourage other central focuses. Nor can they accept Christ as no more than one of many divine manifestations or as merely an historical figure of the past. It is the fullness of Christ, God and man, crucified, risen and ascended which alone meets the needs of Christian contemplative prayer.

In insisting upon this place for the incarnate Lord, Christians must grow in sympathy with their brothers of other traditions who have been brought up in a many-incarnation environment. They are called to make their witness 'with all the meekness and gentleness of Christ.'

In the long run the refusal to compromise the exclusive claims of Christ will be a ministry to the Oriental Schools of Meditation in the West, for their main difficulties and contradictions come from their confusion about the nature of the true Self. When Christ is recognised as this Self, then so

[1] Allison Peers, Trans., *Works of St. John of the Cross*, Vol. 1, p. 176, Burns & Oates and Washburn.

much of the obscurity of their teaching will disappear. For their sakes therefore, as well as for our own integrity, we must guard the treasure of Christ for the day when we can share him fully with our Eastern brothers.

A Modus Vivendi John Macquarrie, in the quotation already referred to, stresses the need for Christians actively to seek closer understanding with other Faiths and urges that a *modus vivendi* should be discovered between them. For us at the Anchorhold,[1] and for all who are taking contemplative prayer seriously, there is a demand for a deeper understanding of our Eastern brothers in their ways of meditation, both in their own countries, and in the adaptations they have made of these ways for the West. Here are some of the many ways this can be done:

First, we must honestly face our differences. They need not be ignored in order for us to have communication, and we need not wait for full reconciliation before we talk in depth with each other. But the main differences must be recognised. Already we have tried to do this. It may be that closer communication will change our assessment of these differences, but we need not try at this stage any verbal cleverness in an effort to reduce or obliterate them.

Secondly, there must be an understanding of our agreements, and they are many. This will make great demands on our sympathy and unprejudiced study. The books and translations for this work are becoming increasingly numerous. What is needed is the willingness to study and communicate.

But most of all the *modus vivendi* will develop as we learn to meditate together. George Appleton in his book on Buddhism recommended that Religious from Christian communities should share in Buddhist community life, which would involve them in shared meditations. Our most moving experience at the Anchorhold was a shared meditation with a Tibetan monk. As we sat together in silence, he brought us the stillness and sorrow of his exile, and reached a unity too deep for words. We have not yet reached the dialogue state of communication with Oriental Meditation

[1] The Anchorhold is a house in Haywards Heath which was given to the Society of St. John the Evangelist. It was then occupied by a member of that Society in January, 1969, and is now being used as a centre of exploration into new ways of community life and contemplative prayer.

Schools and many of us hope we never shall, but the way to corporate meditation with them is already wide open, and in the future we shall hope to share this increasingly. So far as our life at the Anchorhold is concerned, we are sure that neither intellectual nor technical agreement is needed before we can share this *modus vivendi* together.

3

WHAT WE HAVE TO LEARN

IN sending one of its members to the Anchorhold on January 31, 1969, to undertake an exploration into forms of Eastern meditation, the Society of St. John the Evangelist was acting in a great tradition. The Christian Church has always been sensitive to its environment. In the past it borrowed from the Jews, the Greeks and the Romans and it has continued this policy ever since. Now that so much of Eastern thought is being made available in the West and we have such a variety of Oriental Meditation Schools at work, it was appropriate for the 1968 Lambeth Conference to call attention to the need to take notice of this tradition, and to learn and, if necessary, borrow from it.

Those who began this task at the Anchorhold already had some experience of Eastern ways of prayer. During ten years in India, one of them lived in close contact with a Marathi pundit who not only taught his language, but in the process, shared his interpretation of the Yoga system of Patanjali, and later in the West, some experience of Western adaptations of Eastern forms of prayer were a considerable preparation for the work of further exploration. Added to this was the training in a community which has always laid great emphasis on meditation, requiring of its members regular and lengthy practice of this prayer. Much more of course remained to be learnt and experienced, but this was enough to make a beginning and to approach the work with a sense of deep gratitude for the many lessons already given by our Eastern brothers. Before describing part of our own discoveries some brief account of these lessons will be given.

Some Lessons Learnt

First, the importance of meditation. It is true that meditation has been an exercise of many Christians and especially of religious communities, but the Christian Church as a whole in recent times has tended to become increasingly immersed in good works, in theological discussions, in details of ecclesiastical organisation, and in liturgy. Meditation has been left to the few and has lost much of its primitive importance. The Oriental Schools of Meditation have stressed the importance of meditation and many have been surprised at the enthusiastic response they have received, especially among the young. They have confirmed the accuracy of Archbishop Ramsey's judgement when he wrote:

> I believe that the capacity of the ordinary Christian for contemplation is greater by far than some of our theories of the spiritual life have allowed.[1]

The meditation taught by many of the Oriental Meditation Schools has been more than what we should call discursive meditation. They have aimed at what the Archbishop calls 'the capacity for contemplation' in ordinary people. Of course they have described this objective in many ways. The Buddhist has talked of Nirvana, the Hindu of some degree of Samadhi. All have agreed that something more than discursive meditation is what they are calling people to practice, something much nearer the goal described by the Lambeth Conference Report in 1968 in terms of 'learning to keep still and listen to God, fostering each man's capacity for contemplation.'

Again, Oriental Schools of Meditation have reminded the West of the importance of what might be called the 'art' of contemplation. They have also demonstrated this art by drawing up various forms of training techniques. Some of them are obviously unsuitable for people brought up in Western traditions, but at least they make the point that contemplation, like other forms of art, does not happen by chance, but requires planned training for its full development. Others contain important principles that may well be considered by the West and adapted for their needs. These training techniques take into account the body as well as the mind, and

[1] *Canterbury Essays*, p. 29, 1965.

include forms of preparation for each. They also think in terms of training groups where several can share in this experience. Although much of this training assumes a considerable development in prayer, there are also simpler ways for ordinary people, so that they need not be deterred from contemplation and may start from where they are towards the full growth of their contemplative faculties. Not all Oriental Meditation Schools take this detailed care, and some have made the mistake of suggesting that contemplation needs little or no preparation; but enough have set a sound example of contemplative training to be taken seriously. Above all, they have introduced to the West that great master of contemplative prayer, Patanjali, and made his work available as a dependable source book for those who would explore the basic principles of contemplative prayer and training.

In the same year that the Anchorhold was completed, it was the teaching of Patanjali on contemplation which inspired Father J. C. Winslow to produce his own Christian adaptation of this training in a valuable book called *The Art of Contemplation*. In this work he analysed the 'eight limbs' of Patanjali's training and showed how they could be harmonised with the best teaching of Western forms of contemplative prayer. It was this example, together with the lessons given in India on contemplative prayer, which led the small exploration party at the Anchorhold to decide that the Yoga Sutras of Patanjali should be their main written source of the Oriental methods of contemplative prayer. Starting from this point they began with a careful examination of Patanjali's teaching and then, through daily practice as a team, gradually evolved a training programme for contemplative prayer which was found by experience to meet the needs of a young group of contemplative aspirants from the West.

It is always difficult and unsatisfactory to attempt the task of describing what has grown out of corporate movement and trial-and-error experiment, but the Army does not shrink from the task of writing training manuals, and very good they often are. Nor do the teachers of the dance refuse to put its main movements into words. It seems right, therefore, to attempt the task of describing our own experiment of translating some of the teaching of Patanjali in terms of movements designed to train the body and the heart for the supremely demanding work of contemplation. This is the main lesson we have learnt from Oriental forms of meditation, and what follows is an attempt to share our discoveries.

A Form of Training for Contemplation

Patanjali divides his training for contemplation into two parts: a preliminary phase which is designed to establish a sound pattern of harmonious life, and then a detailed form of contemplative training.

The object of both parts is gradually to lessen the strength of the hindrances to contemplation. There are five of these hindrances: blindness, or the lack of awareness of God; egoism; desire; aversion; clinging to life. Patanjali traces four of these hindrances to the first, blindness (avidya). When this is destroyed, then all the other hindrances to contemplation disappear.

The preliminary training is called the Yoga of action (kriya yoga) and consists of the persevering mastery of three forms of discipline: physical austerity, self-study and devotion to God. Through it the power of the hindrances is diminished.

The detailed form of contemplative training is built around what Patanjali calls the 'eight limbs' of Yoga. These may be described as the eight steps towards divine union. They are:

Restraints—observances;

Postures—breathing;

Detachment—concentration;

Meditation—contemplation.

Against the background of this thought and teaching, we have gradually designed a way of life and meditation which adapt the preliminary and advanced training of the Yoga Sutras to a form which fits in with our Christian tradition. It is, of course, provisional and must always be so. What is about to be described is a pattern which is flexible and capable of change to meet the common mind of those who use it. It is a series of principles rather than an unchanging code of rules, and one would hope that such principles would be still further adapted by any other group which might want to use them.

Preliminary Training

The environment of this training is the family which has grown up at the Anchorhold. This family is built around Christ as its centre, and his Spirit as its life. It has a leader, a small nucleus of fairly permanent members, and a varying number of people who come for shorter or longer periods. The evangelical counsels of poverty, chastity and obedience are the principles of the family life, but these are not applied in any legalistic form. They are used as a life-pattern and as a standard for solving the daily problems of living together. The aim of family life is a loving communion with each other in Christ. We welcome him in all who come and make no attempt to pressurise others to conform to a way of prayer to which they are unaccustomed, or find unhelpful. The family does not attempt to withdraw from the world, which is recognised as God's world, the creation which Christ is making a-new, having already reconciled the whole universe to himself. In order to take our full share in this work, the family is involved in training its members in body and heart.

The physical training is concerned with that moderate discipline of the body which leads to health and makes it a responsive instrument of the spirit. Some of the details of this training include, regular and balanced meals, some of the yoga postures, the T'ai Chi Ch'uan,[1] sleep, creative work, and recreation.

The choice of creative work and the performance of it as a way of training the body have been discovered gradually. In the early days we had to build a workshop and then decide what work should be done in it. The decision was made partly on the particular gifts of the family and also on the conviction that it should be work with our hands. At present this work takes the form of woodwork, pottery, weaving and gardening. Should someone else join us with other gifts we should not hesitate to introduce another craft in order to use them.

St. Benedict stressed the importance of co-ordinating prayer and work, but he gave no detailed instructions of the way this should be done. In the teaching of Patanjali there is helpful instruction about this which we have followed. In the third section of the Yoga Sutras he describes the way to bring the mind into a state of concentrated understanding on any particular object. He calls this 'samyama' or mind poise. It consists of three actions

---

[1] The T'ai Chi Ch'uan is a dance of Chinese origin combining mental concentration, deep breathing, balance and gentle physical training.

on a particular object: concentration, meditation and insight. We use this method of concentration in preparing for work. The particular task is first of all isolated and taken into the mind. The mind is then allowed to think around it until it reaches the deepest possible state of imaginative understanding. The hands are then used to carry out the work as it has been thus mentally conceived. This way of praying work is suitable for every manual task and results in the whole attention being pin-pointed upon it. This is an extension of the mental concentration required for the performance of the yoga postures and the T'ai Chi Ch'uan.

Heart training involves the development of two capacities of the heart: its power of thought and its power of love. Of course, these activities overlap, but there is a difference of emphasis in the process of training.

The mental training of the heart is both corporate and individual. The corporate training takes the form of family study of the Greek New Testament, and group readings of spiritual classics, both within and outside the Office.[1] The individual training is through private reading. We are slowly building up our own library, and make full use of the public library. Ample time for this kind of reading is given every day.

The main instrument for training the heart in love is the Office and the Eucharist. The Office is said daily, with two celebrations of the Eucharist during the week, and participation in the parish Eucharist in church on Sundays. This is a demanding form of training for it sifts out the shallower forms of emotion from the greater depths of love. At the same time, it prepares the heart not only for the love of God within itself, but for the practice of that same love towards each other and the whole of Creation. From this discipline grows the energy and material needed to nourish the periods of corporate contemplative prayer which take place after the main parts of the Office each day.

Patanjali insists that growth in contemplation depends upon two things: persevering repetition, and detachment. The regularity of the Office and its detailed planning provide material which can stand the wear and tear of a life-time of repetition, and the absence of unbalanced emotion trains the heart in those ways of detached loving which are essential for its full growth.

[1] The Office is a form of vocal prayer used by the Church. It is made up of hymns, psalms and readings from the Bible. It is said or sung at regular times during the day.

Without the preliminary training which has just been described it would be unwise to embark on contemplative prayer. And without the object of contemplative prayer, the exercises of the preliminary training would be largely superfluous. Both are essential. Patanjali has summarised this contemplative training in his Eight Steps towards union. These, Father J. C. Winslow harmonised with the Western teaching on contemplative prayer. We soon discovered at the Anchorhold that what we needed was not yet another attempt to harmonise this teaching in words, but a form of movement which would express it in terms appropriate to ourselves and also provide us with a form of contemplative training through movement which we could share with each other. The result is what we call a meditation of movement.

The meditation of movement in its present form is a clear-cut pattern of physical and mental exercise which is repeated by the family every day after Terce.[1] Not only does it counteract the physical effects of long sitting in contemplative prayer, but it also provides material for the other meditations during the day. The Patanjali teaching in the Eight Steps is the main source of this meditation of movement, but we are also free to incorporate the dance of movement called the T'ai Chi Ch'uan as an alternative to the Yoga postures. As we regularly use this form we find that it has a power of binding us together as a family and is an effective instrument for introducing others to an understanding of our prayer.

In the meditation of movement all the faculties of our nature are trained: the body, through physical movement; the heart, through concentration and a meditative flow of thought and love; the family, by the subordination of each individual to the leader.

Like the T'ai Chi Ch'uan, the meditation of movement has a theme which acts as a kind of unifying cement to all its parts. This theme is based primarily on the great mysteries of our Lord and our Lady, as they are presented in the Liturgy. The chief parts of this theme are: the annunciation, the visitation, the nativity, the epiphany, the presentation, the temptations, the transfiguration, the crucifixion, the resurrection, the

---

[1] Terce is one of the periods of prayer in the Office. It takes place during the early part of the morning.

ascension and the gift of the Holy Spirit. They are used with considerable freedom, but to guide beginners, we have arranged them in a weekly sequence, together with other details about symbols, on a prayer wheel which has been made in our workshop. Every individual is encouraged to improvise on this scheme as he thinks best.

The meditation of movement takes place in a specially arranged room. This arrangement is planned to be a model of the essential parts of the human body, like the mandala of Eastern prayer. The outside circle, with no more than ten prayer-mats, represents the physical body. The inside circle, with a focal centre made up of a pair of open women's hands, represents the heart as the dwelling place of God. These open hands symbolise the heart in its renewed, receptive relationship with God, and the symbol within them, the theme of the meditation. A bowl of water symbolises the presence of the Holy Spirit.

An Analysis of the Meditation of Movement

There are six sequences in this meditation which are a modified form of Patanjali's Eight Steps. The sequences are: self-denial, turning to Christ, posture, breathing control, detachment, and three acts of contemplation. A leader is required when this meditation is done in a group. The group should normally not be larger than ten. The timing of each movement and the period of stillness in between depend upon the leader, but it has been found helpful to allow some ten complete breaths for each movement.[1]

Sequence 1

Self-Denial Patanjali teaches that contemplation begins with five forms of restraint. These are: restraint from violence, falsehood, theft, incontinence and acquisitiveness. Our Lord's demand is simpler and yet more complete. He sums it up in the invitation: 'Anyone who wishes to be a follower of mine must leave self behind; he must take up his cross, and come with me.' (Mark 8: 34.) This is a call to a complete self-denial, a reordering of our selves. In doing the movements which express this action, some find it helpful to use that description of the old self which is given in the traditional capital sins of envy, gluttony, sloth, anger, pride, covetousness, and lust. We use one of them each day as a point of concentration whilst doing the following acts of self-denial:

[1] See pp. 28–29 for illustrations.

46

1. The vertical posture (tādāsana) with relaxations in the head, throat, heart and abdominal centres
2. Obeisance posture (pāda hastāsana)
3. The vertical posture
4. The meditation walk once round the room in an anti-clockwise direction, using silently the phrase: 'I will walk before the Lord in the land of the living'.
5. The vertical posture.

Sequence II

Turning to Christ Patanjali next demands five observances: purity of body, contentedness, austerity, study, and devotion to God. For the Christian, these are all parts of what is involved in fulfilling the vow of his baptism that he will turn to Christ. This turning to Christ is expressed in move‐ments which are designed to recognise his presence in the heart, in the world and in each other. They are:

6. Three acts of salutation to Christ in the heart (Surya namaskar)
7. The vertical posture
8. The cosmic embrace
9. The vertical posture
10. The kiss of peace, given by the leader and passed round
11. The vertical posture.

Sequence III

The Postures Posture is a translation of the sanskrit word 'āsana' which means a seat or an act of sitting down. Patanjali is mainly interested in the sitting postures for meditation. He does not say which they are, but leaves his pupils free to select the ones most suitable. He does however lay down these principles for the meditation posture: (a) it should be steady and comfortable, (b) it is reached by relaxation and concentration on God, and (c) it is a state of balanced tension.

In order to reach the right meditation posture, some kind of training is needed and this is supplied by a selection of a few from the many yoga postures which are available. The following are the ones we have found most useful. We use them to train the body and mind to reach a tension-relaxation state, one which has been carefully analysed by Dr. Ainslie Meares in his valuable book, *Relief without Drugs*. Of this tension-relaxation state he writes:

47

The aim is more complete relaxation of the mind. When we are in comfortable positions the relaxation of our mind comes largely from the feeling of bodily comfort. When we achieve this relaxation in situations of physical discomfort, the relaxation comes from the mind itself.[1]

These postures have a two-fold effect—they discipline the physical body, and they develop the spiritual body.

The horizontal (12) posture (savāsana) is used as the relaxation posture between each of the āsanas. Then follow:

13. Shoulder-stand (sarvāngāsana)
14. Plough (halāsana)
15. Backstretch (paschimottānāsana)
16. Cobra (bhujangāsana)
17. Head-stand (shirāsana)
18. Folded leaf (virāsana).

As an alternative to this series of postures, the T'ai Chi Ch'uan is regularly done in groups of not more than three people.

Sequence IV

Breath Control Breath is a translation of the sanskrit word 'prana'. This means much more than air; it refers to the spiritual energy of the universe and corresponds to what we mean by the word Spirit. The instrument for receiving and using this energy is what St. Paul calls the spiritual body. In the Vedanta teaching, this instrument is called the pranayama kosha. Since physical breathing and co-operation with the Spirit are closely related, breath control begins with regulation of the breathing. There are three breathing movements: expiration (rechaka), inspiration (puraka) and restraint (kumbhaka). The object of breath control is the restraint of the breathing whilst keeping the attention upon the work and presence of the Spirit. We find it helpful to think of the Spirit infusing the virtues of justice, moderation, courage, prudence, faith, hope and love. Also to meditate on his work in our Lady and the Church through the mysteries of the conception, annunciation, visitation, presentation at the cross, the resurrection and in glory. Other material for meditation on his work is supplied by the sevenfold gift of wisdom, understanding, knowledge, counsel, spiritual strength, true godliness and holy fear. Each individual

[1] *ibid*, p. 106.

48

makes his own choice of subjects, whilst sharing in the following acts which are practised thus:

19. Assume one of the meditation postures.

20. Clear the nasal passages by breathing through each nostril separately, using a regular rhythm for the breathing movements of expiration, restraint, inspiration, restraint, and expiration.

21. Continue this breathing rhythm for some ten or twenty seconds, using, if helpful, a simple repetitive phrase such as 'Inspire our hearts with your Holy Spirit'.

Sequence V

Detachment This is a preparation of the heart for contemplation. It is an exercise in draining off distractions and withdrawing the senses from outside stimulation. Our Lord described the life of the heart in this way: 'Out of man's heart come evil thoughts, acts of fornication, of theft, murder, adultery, ruthless greed and malice; fraud, indecency, envy, slander, arrogance and folly'. (Mark 7: 21–22) This exercise in detachment assists this draining of the heart by allowing these impurities to run away and by stopping the sources of renewal.

22. Stand in the vertical posture with the arms crossed.

23. Allow the thoughts to run freely, recognise them and reject them.

24. Withdraw the senses from all outside objects and concentrate them inwardly.

Sequence VI

Contemplative Acts Patanjali defined the object of his contemplative discipline as the control of the images in the heart. He went on to trace the source of these images in terms of right and wrong knowledge. Right knowledge, he taught, was derived from direct observation (pratyaksha), correct reasoning (anumāna) and dependable tradition (agama). He also traced the source of wrong knowledge in terms of a distortion between the fact and the mental image made to represent it. To achieve control of the images in the heart, Patanjali required persevering practice of certain forms of mental discipline and detachment. The mental discipline required was concentration on a single object, a flow of thought called meditation around it, and then identification with the reality represented by the object of concentration. When the object of concentration had completed its task of steadying the mind, he insisted that it should be removed so that the most complete state of contemplation would be imageless and a complete unity of consciousness with God. All this Patanjali worked out in great practical detail. We have chosen from his analysis what we have found necessary for our own acts of contemplation. Two things are needed: an object on which to concentrate, and a theme to stimulate the mind to a flow of thought around it.

Because the world is God's workmanship we have felt free to choose any created thing as an object of concentration. This can appeal to any of the senses—a visual object, a smell, sound, or an object of touch or taste. In practice, however, in order to simplify our selection of concentration objects, we have found it best to limit our choice to the image material given in the Bible, or in the ceremonies of the Church.

Any meditation theme which conforms to St. Paul's standards in Philippians (4: 8, is equally legitimate, but here again we have found some kind of limitation helpful, and so have used the incarnate mysteries of our Lord as the normal meditation themes.

This has led us to draw up a repetitive scheme of concentration objects and meditative themes which form the usual material for our contemplative acts and so far it has not worn out. If it does, we shall not hesitate to modify it. Even now we alter it when some important commemoration in the Office occurs.

SCHEME OF CONCENTRATION

	Concentration object	*Meditation theme*
Monday	Water	Annunciation
Tuesday	Star	Epiphany
Wednesday	Cross	Temptations
Thursday	Bread	Transfiguration
Friday	Chalice	Crucifixion
Saturday	Candle	Resurrection
Sunday	Crown	Ascension

Patanjali gives the following alternative meditation themes and we draw on them when needed: breathing; an absorbing sense experience; the peaceful inner light of the heart; the lives of the saints; dreams; sleep; any congenial subject; the Lord. These have their place in our own meditations as variations from the ordinary scheme.

The following movements are used to express the contemplative acts:

25. Stand in the vertical posture and stretch the right hand towards the central object of concentration. Bring all the senses into focus upon it.

26. Move to the centre using the meditation walk.

27. Standing at the centre, put the hands in the receptive posture, close the eyes and make an image of the object of concentration in the heart.

28. Return to the circumference, holding the image in the heart centre and direct the mind, by means of an appropriate phrase, to think around the image whilst standing in the vertical posture.

29. Relax in the tree posture (vrikshasana) and then, using the meditation walk, move once round the room, keeping the mind in a flow of thought around the image. A short phrase relating to the meditation theme is helpful, repeated in silence.

30. Relax in the vertical posture. Do the tree posture. Then sit in the meditation posture and erase the image from the heart, relaxing in an inner and loving silence centred upon the divine Lord in the heart. Make acts of loving reception and loving giving in harmony with the breathing rhythm. If the attention wanders, remake the image in the heart and then gently erase it and return to the silence.

This climax of the contemplative acts cannot be fully described and verbal description should not be attempted. St. Paul has adequately hinted at its meaning: 'The life I now live is not my life but the life which Christ lives in me.' (Gal. 2: 20) That is all we know and all we need to know.

Other Meditation Forms

We are learning at the Anchorhold to apply some of the principles of the contemplative acts to other forms of prayer, especially to the Eucharist, the Office and Intercession.

In the Eucharist we have introduced the contemplative acts into the revised form of this service. We use both the Bible and the bread and wine as objects of concentration, and have periods of silence when the mind can think around them and open into contemplative awareness. We also use the meditation walk with the psalms. Certain hand gestures have also been found helpful.

In the Office we make use of the meditation postures for reciting the psalms, and we intersperse the prayers with silence. After the morning Office, terce and evensong we follow the prayers with half-an-hour of corporate meditation.

In his book *The Foolishness of God* John Austin Baker writes of intercessory prayer as follows:

> In technical terms, intercession is a form of that kind of prayer known as contemplation, with the special feature that here we contemplate not God in himself but God in his relationship of love towards those whom we also love.[1]

Our own search into intercessory prayer has led us to the same conclusion. We have followed the clue given in the Collects where the petitionary part of the prayer is based upon an attribute or act of God. Taking one of his revealed actions, and using a symbol to express this action, we perform the three acts of contemplation already described, and in identifying ourselves with God, share in the communication of his Spirit to those for whom we pray. We are still feeling our way in this form of contemplation but one of the daily periods of contemplative prayer is given to the practice of this form of intercession. It seems to follow the pattern set by our Lord in his prayer in Gethsemane where, using the chalice as an image of concentration, he allowed his thoughts to flow around it, and then brought his will into union with the Father's and was strengthened to go out and be the instrument of its fulfilment.

[1] *ibid*, p. 386.

4

POINTS TO REMEMBER

IF you are invited to join in Oriental Meditation, here are some questions to ask, and some important distinctions to make.

1. What is meditation ?

Meditation is a form of silent prayer. In Oriental meditation this often takes the form of repeating a word or phrase called a *mantra*. In Christian meditation it often takes the form of thinking about some event or teaching in the life of our Lord.

2. What is contemplation ?

Contemplation is a developed form of meditation in which the mind is held in silence. Oriental forms of contemplation emphasise the absence of ordinary thought processes and stillness. Christian contemplation is concerned with the present life of our Lord in glory. It also aims at silence, stillness and loving union with him.

3. What is self-realisation ?

This is a term often found in Oriental forms of meditation. It is vague insofar as the true Self is equated with the creative principle at the centre of one's being. Most often this means the Oriental conception of God. Christian self-realisation has been summed up by St. Paul: 'I have been crucified with Christ: the Life I now live is not my life, but the life which

Christ lives in me: and my present bodily life is lived by faith in the Son of God, who loved me and sacrificed himself for me.' (Gal. 2: 20. N.E.B.)

4. What techniques of meditation are being suggested ?

There are many ways of meditating, depending upon the tradition of the teacher and the capacity of the pupil. Some Oriental Schools of Meditation stress the simplicity of the technique and the possibility of its being easily mastered by anyone. Patanjali on the other hand demands considerable preparation and training. Christian forms of meditation vary from the simplicity of the 'Jesus Prayer' to the detailed method of the Ignatian Exercises.

5. Is it a true form of meditation that suggests retreat from the world ?

Christians are expected to combine meditation with their work, though they are also encouraged to take part in more intense periods of meditation by withdrawing from their ordinary work for a few days and taking part in a retreat.

6. Is the purpose of meditation to help the person meditating or to help other people ?

Christian teaching about the communion of saints claims that the good things received by holy people are available for all, and that when a member of a community is spiritually awake he will share his enlightenment with others, thus bringing light and strength to himself at the same time.

7. What is the object of meditation and the power by which it is used ?

For the Christian the object of meditation is God as revealed in Jesus Christ and the power of meditation is his Holy Spirit.

8. What literature is being suggested as an aid to meditation ?

All true literature is a help to meditation since it provides food for the mind. Oriental forms of meditation derive much help from such writings as the *Bhagavad Gita*. Christians believe that the Bible is the Word of God and the source of our true thinking about him.